The CBCT® for Educators

Implementation Guide

Bringing Compassion Training into Education Systems

Center for Contemplative
Science and Compassion-Based Ethics
Emory University

Contents

Introduction

This guide offers a thoughtful approach for implementing compassion training within education systems to foster and sustain a culture of compassion and a greater sense of wellbeing in educators, students, and all members of the education system.

CBCT® (Cognitively Based Compassion Training) is a research-based program that aims to enhance wellbeing through the cultivation of resilience and compassion. The most researched compassion training program to date, CBCT has been shown to improve both personal and social wellbeing factors in participants. Through the cultivation of competencies including resilience, awareness, discernment, and compassion, CBCT® for Educators can help to reduce educators' physical and emotional symptoms of burnout, increase teacher retention, strengthen academic outcomes and student engagement, support educators in navigating challenging situations with students or colleagues, and contribute to a greater sense of connection and meaning in the workplace.

Given the limited resources education systems have to meet students' many needs (behavioral, academic, social, emotional, psychological, etc.), investing time, resources, and money into staff wellbeing can seem misplaced. However, research studies support the idea that an educator's efficacy and relationship with their students are significant factors in a student's academic achievement and wellbeing.[1] Investing in the wellbeing of educators is also investing in the wellbeing of students.

This implementation guide is designed to support the integration of CBCT for Educators into education systems, including elementary, secondary, and higher education settings. The implementation process outlined in this guide, involves a thoughtful approach to deepen understanding of the needs of the school and readiness for this compassion training program, to explore the best way to offer the training to different community members within the system, and to integrate the practices and skills into existing structures to contribute to long-term benefits.

Through the development of a deliberative and thoughtful plan, and a commitment over time to executing it, CBCT for Educators can be implemented in a manner that contributes to a more caring school culture, enhances the wellbeing and effectiveness of educators, and promotes the flourishing and success of students.

"Compassion is essential for survival. Without cooperation, trust, gratitude, and reciprocity—as well as the many other qualities associated with compassion—humans would not have survived, let alone flourished."

— Dacher Keltner, *Born to Be Good: The Science of a Meaningful Life,* 2009

Program Overview

CBCT, a program of Emory University's Center for Contemplative Science and Compassion-Based Ethics (colloquially, the Compassion Center), is a comprehensive and research-based compassion training protocol. Professor Lobsang Tenzin Negi, PhD developed CBCT in 2004, drawing from the ancient Indo-Tibetan Buddhist teachings of *lojong* along with complementary insights from emotion science to create this multi-layered and practical approach.

As the most researched compassion training program of its kind, CBCT has contributed to a growing body of research linking compassion training to greater resilience and well-being. Studies suggest that compassion training not only lowers stress hormones and strengthens immune response, but it also decreases rumination, activates pleasure circuits in the brain, increases self-reported happiness, fosters more optimistic and supportive communication styles, and serves as an antidote to burnout. CBCT has had a transformative impact on educators, healthcare providers, spiritual health practitioners, military veterans with post-traumatic stress disorder, adolescents in foster care, parents of children with autism, transgender youth and their parents, breast cancer survivors, and many others.

Professor Negi developed CBCT in response to a plea from an undergraduate student at Emory who was committed to supporting her campus community amidst a mental health crisis. When taking a course taught by Professor Negi, she found that the practices he presented, on cultivating resilience and self-compassion and enhancing a sense of belonging and warm-hearted connection to others, could be just what her fellow students needed. Her encouragement led Professor Negi to develop CBCT as a program for people of any or no faith tradition, designed to help participants cultivate inner skills and perspective that contribute to greater flourishing.

CBCT Research Outcomes

Significant decreases in:

- stress biomarkers and inflammatory response[2]
- depression[3]
- loneliness[4]
- PTSD symptoms[5]

Significant increases in:

- hopefulness[6]
- compassion and related neural activity[7]
- empathy and related neural activity[8]
- self-compassion[9]

For published research on the above outcomes, visit *compassion.emory.edu*.

26
Countries Represented by Teachers

15
Languages

300+
Certified Teachers

15
Certified Senior Teachers

6,000+
Full Course Participants

15
Introduced to CBCT

How Does CBCT Stand Out From Other Programs?

▶ CBCT holds the distinction of being one of the longest-running and most studied compassion protocols of its kind.

▶ CBCT is linked to improvements in health and wellbeing across studies.

▶ Rather than a one-size-fits-all approach, CBCT has been tailored to various sectors, including education, healthcare, business, and for mental health practitioners, by experts in their respective fields—all with impressive results.

▶ CBCT forms the cornerstone of the Compassion Shift®, a global initiative that aims to advance a global culture of compassion.

▶ CBCT for Educators, when combined with SEE Learning® (Social, Emotional and Ethical Learning), allows educators and students to learn alongside each other and foster a greater culture of compassion.

Learn more about the Compassion Shift initiative at: *compassionshift. emory.edu.*

CBCT for Educators

In 2024, Emory's Compassion Center launched a uniquely tailored program—CBCT for Educators—for those who teach and work in schools.

CBCT for Educators is a novel approach to professional wellbeing that is directed at the whole person. It is designed to equip educators with practices that support a greater sense of empowerment, efficacy, and connection as they move through their work and personal lives.

Adapted in recognition of the importance of a systems approach to wellness and culture change, CBCT for Educators was also specifically developed to contribute to the wellbeing of students by supporting a teacher's knowledge and expertise in SEL. As teachers learn and practice these skills, they can become models for their students. The educators' personal practice also leads to subtle (and sometimes not-so-subtle) changes in their emotional and social intelligence. The practices are designed to naturally shift small interactions—like the use of language, tone of voice, or gestures—that can make a world of difference to individual students and to classrooms as a whole. These shifts may not all be conscious to the teacher or the student, but neuroscience tells us that we pick up on these subtle signals even unconsciously, and they can shape our levels of trust and confidence with each other. As a strong sense of safety and trust grows in the classroom, this can have a tremendous impact on student learning. And as educators reinforce these essential practices for their students, they are simultaneously improving their own wellbeing and their efficacy as classroom teachers or administrators.

CBCT for Educators is designed to work hand in hand with SEE Learning® (Social, Emotional, and Ethical Learning), a program for students also developed at Emory's Compassion Center. Together, CBCT and SEE Learning are part of the Compassion Shift initiative, which aims to promote human flourishing by advancing a global culture of compassion.

Learn More about CBCT for Educators

Training Compassion for Educators: The Official Guide to CBCT® for Educators (2025).

Compassion U™, the digital learning platform for all CBCT courses. The Compassion U website shares information on the CBCT program, courses, and how to bring it to your school or organization: *compassionu. app*

The Challenges Facing Educators

Educator Burnout and Attrition

According to a national poll, school-based educators are experiencing the highest rate of burnout among all fields consulted. 44 percent of educators report experiencing burnout. The bottom line is that educators represent "a workforce that is burned out and unfortunately leaving the profession at a high rate."[10]

The United Nations has issued a global alert regarding the issue of teacher retention. The United Nations Secretary-General has stated that "now, more than ever, we need to move towards learning societies. People everywhere need high quality skills, knowledge, and education. Above all, they need the best teachers possible."[11] Teacher shortages affect communities around the world, and addressing the issue of teacher retention is essential for meeting students' educational needs. The research[12] identifies that improved collaboration, support from their school's administration, and an educators sense of self-agency[13] all serve to address issues of teacher retention.

CBCT for Educators can serve as an effective tool for addressing factors influencing educator burnout and attrition. It provides a platform for educators and administrators to promote self-agency and wellbeing through the development of greater resilience, self-compassion, and discernment, and by fostering more meaningful relationships in the workplace.

Chronic Absenteeism

Chronic absenteeism, defined as when a student misses at least 10 percent of school days, is one of the most significant issues facing schools. Research shows that chronic absenteeism negatively impacts a student's academic achievement and performance on standardized tests.[14] It is also a significant predictor of dropping out of high school,[15] which in turn predicts poor employment prospects,[16] diminished health,[17] and an increased involvement in the criminal justice system.[18]

Addressing chronic absenteeism requires students to cultivate a sense of belonging and engagement at school. One of the best ways to achieve this is to support the healthy relationships shared between a student and their teacher.[19] Through the development of greater resilience and compassion, CBCT for Educators can support teachers in navigating the challenges of chronic absenteeism and fostering more meaningful connections with their students.

Student Mental Health Crisis

Mental Health Data (US Data—National Alliance for Mental Health)

- 1 in 5 US adults experience mental illness each year.
- 1 in 20 US adults experience serious mental illness each year.
- 1 in 6 US youth aged 6–17 experience a mental health disorder each year.
- 50 percent of all lifetime mental illness begins by age 14, and 75 percent by age 24.
- Suicide is the second leading cause of death among people aged 10–14.

US High School Students (CDC Youth Risk Behavior Survey)

- In 2021, more than 4 out of 10 (42 percent) students felt persistently sad or hopeless and nearly 3 out of 10 (29 percent) experienced poor mental health.
- In 2021, more than 1 out of 5 (22 percent) students seriously considered attempting suicide and 1 out of 10 (10 percent) attempted suicide.

University Student Mental Health Data (Global Data—World Health Organization)

- About 1 out of 3 college freshmen reported having suffered from mental health disorders prior to attending college.
- During the 2020–2021 school year, more than 60 percent of college students met the criteria for at least one mental health problem.
- 1 in 5 college students reported having suicidal thoughts in 2018.
- 64 percent of college drop-outs cite a mental health-related reason for leaving college. Furthermore, 45 percent of these students did not report their mental health struggles before deciding to leave college.

Since its development, SEE Learning has reached more than 7 million children and has been adopted by education systems in more than 40 countries, from India to Ukraine, and from Brazil to Mongolia.

Learn more at *seelearning.emory.edu*

"We're learning how to build relationships, and even more to be more reflective in our practices, from learning how to meditate with Cognitively Based Compassion Training . . . It pushes me to be really reflective, but also it makes me be a better educator."

— TRACEY PENDLEY, GEORGIA'S 2020 TEACHER OF THE YEAR

Alignment with SEE Learning

In 2015, Professor Negi was asked by the Dalai Lama to develop a framework and curricula for secular ethics to be implemented in schools around the world. Professor Negi led a team of trained CBCT instructors to design the framework. The team drew heavily on their CBCT training, as well as their prior experience in adapting the meditative protocol for elementary school-age children. This program came to be known as SEE Learning, a program that provides educators with age-appropriate curricula that offer tools and practices to support student wellbeing.

As recommended by CASEL, the building of adult SEL capacity is a critical step in the successful implementation of student-focused SEL or related wellness programming. Emory University's SEE Learning program is recommended by CASEL, having achieved CASEL SELect status for all grade levels.

SEE Learning aligns with CBCT for Educators in important ways, as both programs are anchored by their respective and overlapping learning outcomes, referred to as Enduring Capabilities. The implementation of CBCT for Educators for faculty and staff and SEE Learning for students provides a comprehensive, research-based program that promotes wellbeing throughout the entire school community, through the development of competencies, including awareness, resilience, and compassion for the self and others.

History of CBCT Implementation in Education

Implementation of CBCT at Emory University

The implementation of CBCT in educational contexts began at Emory University, where CBCT was developed in 2004. Since its inception, CBCT has been offered to hundreds of Emory students. It has been folded into undergraduate courses housed in the Human Health and Religion departments, offered as a 1-credit course through the Health and Physical Education department, and as a free course for undergraduate and graduate students, co-sponsored by Emory's Counseling and Psychological Services (CAPS).

CBCT has been brought to staff, faculty, and senior leadership at Emory through course offerings and workshops. In some cases, this has led individuals and whole departments to complete their CBCT teacher certification and begin offering the course to others in the community.

Healthcare education at Emory is one area that has heavily integrated CBCT into their schools and programs. Two examples of this implementation are described below.

Emory School of Medicine: In 2014, the leaders of the Emory School of Medicine invited Professor Negi to teach a comprehensive CBCT course to 20 of the school's top leaders, including Dean Christian Larsen, MD. From this, Dean Larsen and other leaders—including Executive Dean of Education William J. Eley, MD, and Associate Dean of Students Ira Schwartz, MD— became convinced that CBCT could serve as an antidote to a number of the common struggles that plague physicians and seem to begin during their medical training, including depersonalization, depression, suicidality, and anxiety.

The interest that this generated led to Dean Larsen's funding of a randomized control trial—led by veteran CBCT researcher and medical anthropologist, Jennifer Mascaro, PhD—that tailored CBCT for

"The work I've been doing with CBCT has been life-changing. I see and walk in the world differently. I like to think I am less likely to contribute to systems of oppression. I find myself revitalized and ready to stay in the classroom when I thought I was about to quit."

—EDUCATOR AND CBCT PARTICIPANT

"Understanding that my inward work will help me help others was critical. I have tapped into an energy that will help me navigate through the spirals of being an educator during a very challenging time. I have tools that will allow me to recalibrate myself . . ."

— EDUCATOR AND CBCT PARTICIPANT

second-year medical students and showed a significant increase in compassion and decreases in loneliness, sleep disturbances, and depression symptoms. For more than 10 years now, Emory's Compassion Center has successfully taught CBCT to hundreds of Emory physicians and physicians-in training, as well as to genetic counselors, physical therapists, nurses, and physician's assistants, via this partnership.

Emory Spiritual Health: In 2016, another partnership bloomed with Emory Healthcare, this time with the Department of Spiritual Health, which oversees the hospital chaplains and houses one of the largest hospital- chaplaincy training programs in the United States. The leadership in Spiritual Health, especially Executive Director George Grant, PhD, and Director of Education Maureen Shelton, MDiv, had been searching for a training program that would address the emerging and changing needs for hospital chaplains—especially the real need to serve an increasingly diverse population of patients and staff who bring with them a widening variety of beliefs and traditions. They found CBCT's approach promising from the start, thanks to its emphasis on values and ethics and its alignment with many people's understanding of spirituality, while also respecting the beliefs of all major faith traditions.

At first, CBCT was folded into chaplaincy education, but soon the chaplains began to report using their CBCT practices to support active patient and staff encounters. From these insights, Compassion-Centered Spiritual Health (CCSH™) was established and soon evolved into a formal training curriculum that builds on CBCT to bolster the wellbeing, resilience, and compassion of healthcare patients and staff. This generative collaboration between Emory University's Spiritual Health at the Woodruff Health Sciences Center and Emory's Compassion Center augments spiritual health education and best practices with CBCT. CCSH interventions are delivered by spiritual care professionals trained in both CBCT and ACPE: The Standard in Spiritual Care and Education. Emory now trains chaplains internationally and certifies them as CCSH Registered Clinicians. See *ccsh.emory.edu* for more information.

Implementation of CBCT in Atlanta Public Schools

Emory's Compassion Center collaborated with the Atlanta Public Schools and Georgia State University in the implementation of CREATE (Collaboration and Reflection to Enhance Atlanta Teacher Effectiveness), a three-pronged effort to increase teacher wellness, effectiveness, and retention that provided intensive support to new teachers.

The CREATE residency integrated CBCT into new-teacher induction in a number of ways across the 16 school campuses where it operated. First, CBCT was a required core course for all teacher residents in the first year of their three-year programming. Across the school year, one CBCT module per month (for a total of nine sessions, including the Overview) was taught at the beginning of a full day of professional development training. Recordings of guided formal practices were provided to support practice between classes, and informal practices were identified and encouraged. In addition, teachers at each campus formed small groups that met every other week as professional-development communities. Those meetings began with a recorded CBCT meditation based on the module that the teachers had learned that month, as well as a chance to share a personal reflection or insight based on CBCT content. CBCT was also offered separately each semester as an option to mentor teachers, administrators, and parents in the school community, typically weekly after school for nine weeks or as a two-weekend intensive course. Some schools introduced the CBCT settling practice as a way to begin all-staff meetings and brought age-appropriate adaptations of CBCT concepts and practices into student body meetings.

Though unsettling nationwide statistics have consistently shown that nearly half of all new Black teachers in US cities leave the teaching profession within three years of starting, those in this program had quite different outcomes. An external evaluation of the CREATE project found that the program significantly improved Black residents' stress management, empathy, resilience, and self-efficacy, and that more than 95 percent of Black residents had chosen to remain in the field for at least five years—statistics that garnered significant attention from the US Department of Education.[20]

Qualitative studies gathered numerous responses from Black teachers in the program, reporting how CBCT helped them to find the strength and creativity needed to navigate the emotional and physical challenges of beginning a career as a teacher. Common outcomes included being more aware of their emotional sparks before they grew into fires; being able to handle setbacks and mistakes without engaging in overly harsh self-criticism; investing in relationships with other educators to create community support; and learning ways to bring all students—including those facing (and bringing to the classroom) the most significant challenges—into their circle of concern.

"I thought this work was designed to help me as a teacher, but I am so happy because I feel like the course really helped me as a person first and the teacher part of me will only benefit."

— EDUCATOR WITH CREATE

"While I believe I already have a great capacity for empathy both in my professional and personal lives, I look for any opportunity to expand and hone these skills. I'm particularly interested in ways I can use these skills to better support my students while preventing burnout for myself."

— UM FACULTY MEMBER

"Overall, these practices have benefited me both personally and professionally. I am able to navigate through stressful situations a bit easier, taking time to reflect on treating others the way I would want to be treated and deferring from negative judgment. These practices have helped me to pause those negative feelings about myself. This is the first time I feel like I can be successful in loving myself!"

— UM STAFF MEMBER

Implementation of CBCT at the University of Montana

In efforts to implement CBCT at the University of Montana, a certified CBCT instructor met with the provost to discuss the potential for CBCT to contribute to the wellbeing of the faculty and staff and help cultivate a greater culture of compassion. Thereafter, a CBCT course was offered for the deans of the university in the summer of 2022. In collaboration with the Office of Staff Development, this same course was provided in the fall of 2022 to UM staff and faculty. This hybrid course consisted of nine sessions, two of which occurred in person on the UM campus. A second CBCT course was offered in the spring of 2023. At that time, two members of the UM community were invited to join the CBCT Teacher Certification program. The feedback and engagement from UM staff and faculty within these pilot programs demonstrated both interest and personal benefit. Some of the motivations noted by those who joined the course included combating burnout and stress, cultivating tools to better support students, restoring feelings of balance, and supporting personal mental health and wellbeing. Upon completing the course, faculty and staff reported feeling calmer and less reactive, and they appreciated having the tools to better manage stress and navigate challenging situations. Other benefits they noted included improved sleep, enhanced compassion for others, and greater self-love.

"We've seen many changes among the students (preservice teachers), both in their attitudes and decision-making. They immediately adapt the topics to their lives. I've seen a very positive change in their opinions before and after the subject."

— INSTRUCTOR OF CBCT COURSE FOR PRESERVICE TEACHERS

Implementation of CBCT for Preservice Teachers in Mexico

Many SEE Learning educators have seen the value of bringing CBCT to educators and have started offering and implementing CBCT in education systems. In one example, a SEE Learning affiliate in Mexico endeavored to bring CBCT to preservice teachers to further support adult SEL.

CASEL and other organizations have published numerous reports emphasizing the importance of adult SEL, particularly for educators. Effective adult SEL programs can enhance educators' wellbeing, positively impacting their interactions and relationships with students in the classroom.

Since early 2020, this SEE Learning affiliate in Mexico has forged strong ties with the Teacher College of Monclova (Normal de Monclova) and introduced CBCT as a foundational course for developing adult SEL skills. This course serves as a precursor to training focused on teaching social–emotional skills in the classroom. Participants in the foundational CBCT course have reported positive impacts, noting benefits both personally and in their teaching practices.

"This course has been beneficial to me because I consider myself a very anxious person who easily gets stressed by the various daily activities, including college. The practices have helped me find a calm and resilient zone. This is essential as a future teacher because, when we are well, we can help students navigate life's challenges."

— PRESERVICE TEACHER, POST-CBCT FOR EDUCATORS COURSE

Implementation Process

A cohesive plan for implementing CBCT for Educators in schools goes beyond offering one class or training. Implementation involves a thoughtful approach to bringing CBCT for Educators to a school community and system in a way that meets the specific needs of each group and individual, allowing the program greater opportunities to be integrated in meaningful and sustainable ways. This section walks through four key components to consider in the implementation process.

The Four Components
of CBCT for Educators' Implementation

1		Set the Foundation	Lay the groundwork for the implementation of CBCT for Educators.
2		Engage the Community	Introduce CBCT for Educators to the community to create buy-in, and collaborate with stakeholders to make a plan for implementation.
3		Offer the Training	Offer the Training Compassion for Educators course.
4		Support Ongoing Integration	Sustain and integrate CBCT for Educators.

Component 1
Set the Foundation

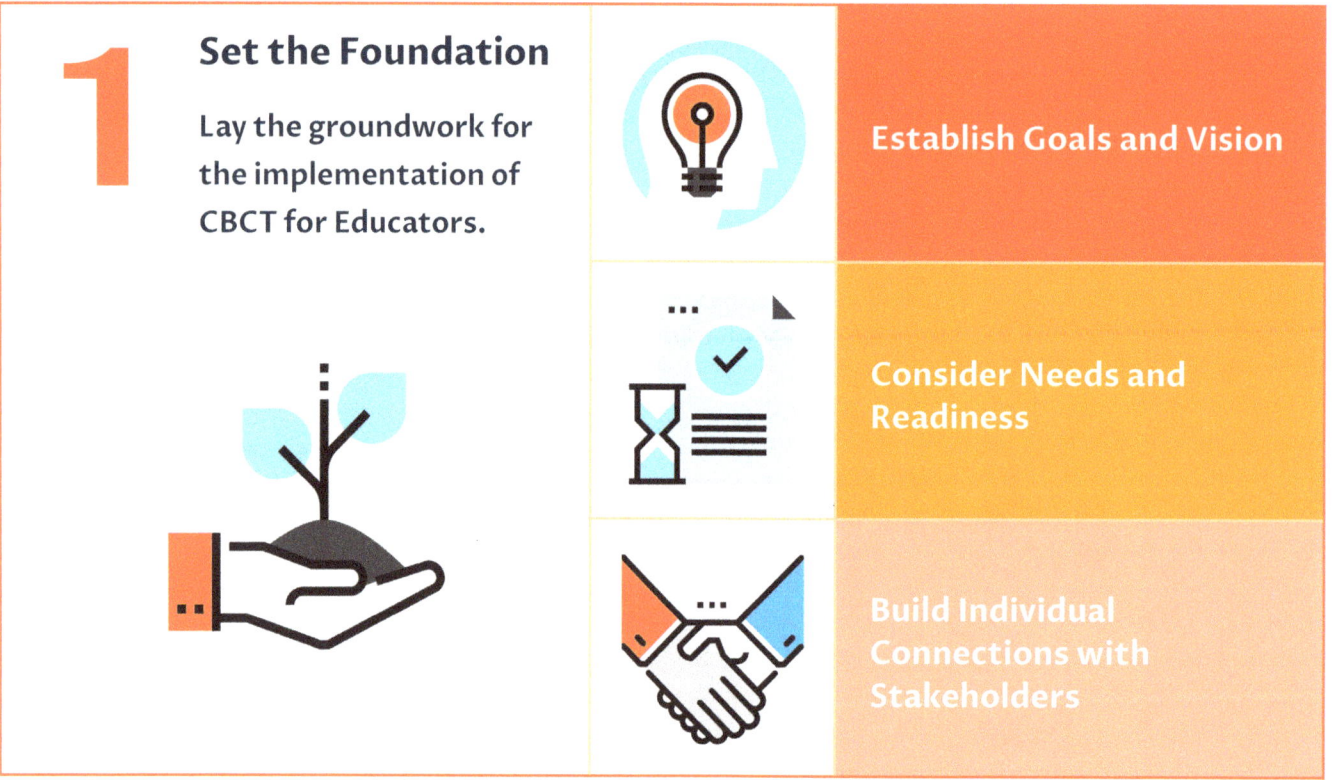

Set the Foundation

Lay the groundwork for the implementation of CBCT for Educators.

Establish Goals and Vision

Consider Needs and Readiness

Build Individual Connections with Stakeholders

 ## Establish Goals and Vision

Before formally engaging in the implementation work, consider the following guiding questions. If there is a team spearheading the implementation of CBCT for Educators, a meeting should be held to discuss these points as a group and come to agreed-upon goals and direction.

Through the consideration of these questions, the individual or group should be able to identify and articulate the main goals of implementation and put together a brief description of the vision.

Guiding Questions – Establish Goals and Vision	What does CBCT for Educators have to offer this community?
	What are the main goals of implementing CBCT for Educators here?
	Can you identify specific shifts that implementation would lead to in the community? What are the desired outcomes?
	How does CBCT for Educators differ from other programs or initiatives?
	How does the implementation of CBCT for Educators fit into the school's vision or goals? How does this work align with the school's existing values and culture?

 ## Consider Needs and Readiness

Determining the school's readiness for CBCT implementation is essential because no two school systems are the same. This involves reflecting on the current school climate and conditions for implementation, including capacity, resources, assets, and needs. This process builds on the vision and goals-setting reflection to support leaders in making decisions about CBCT training options and implementation structures.

The following questions are designed to support an individual or group as they begin to consider the school's needs and their readiness for CBCT implementation.

Guiding Questions – Consider Needs and Readiness

How do you expect CBCT to be perceived? Do you know if your staff is experiencing new-initiative fatigue?

What needs does your education system have that this work might support? What do you want to focus on improving?

Describe the overall staff morale. What considerations need to be made to support, improve, and/or sustain the current culture and climate?

What is already in place (wellness programming, health initiatives, team building activities, staff appreciation events, etc.) that can be built upon to support this work?

Do the educators have professional development time available to them?

What financial, human, and physical resources are available to plan and support training and implementation?

What do you have the capacity to commit to? What will be needed to sustain the work?

Are there groups or individuals you can identify as potential early adopters of CBCT for Educators (e.g., individuals who may already be interested or would be more likely to express interest)?

Build Individual Connections with Stakeholders

It is important to begin conversions with stakeholders, including individuals who would be able to support this work and those who may be interested in engaging in the training and/or implementation of CBCT for Educators. Starting these conversations early helps to set the foundation for this work to succeed. Depending on the organization, stakeholders could consist of:

Building connections with these people and groups could occur through one-on-one meetings, small-group presentations, or other targeted engagement efforts.

Component 2
Engage the Community

2 **Engage the Community**

Introduce CBCT for Educators to the community to create buy-in, and collaborate with stakeholders to make a plan for implementation.

	Offer an Orientation Session
	Form the CBCT Committee
	Conduct a Stakeholder Audit
	Develop and Execute an Outreach and Communication Plan

Offer an Orientation Session

The orientation session aims to introduce CBCT for Educators to those who are likely to be interested in being part of the implementation process. The goal of this session is to orient them to the CBCT for Educators program, highlight the value of implementing the program into their education system, and explain the ways they can get involved to support that work. These sessions are typically one to two hours.

Orientation Session Content

An Overview of CBCT for Educators (~15 min)

This section will cover an exploration of CBCT's framework and history, its benefits for educators, its approach to cultivating resilience and wellbeing, and the science that supports it.

The Implementation Process (~30 min)

This section goes over the goals of implementation, options for implementation, possible next steps, and community engagement possibilities. When describing this process, consider the following:

- Articulate a clear alignment to the education system's vision and mission.
- Articulate a clear "why" and "what" statement for CBCT implementation.
- Be authentic about your personal investment in CBCT.
- Make connections between CBCT and similar methods that are part of your school's culture, such as SEL, restorative practices, trauma-informed practices, or any other programs that are utilized by your school/organization.
- Highlight how CBCT stands out. What makes CBCT different?
- Discuss the challenges and opportunities that may arise from implementing this program.
- Acknowledge the rise and fall of education reform and take time to hear and address concerns about this.
- Mention that there will be an invitation to join a CBCT committee for those interested in being involved with the implementation process.

Discussion and Collaboration (~15 min)

Lastly, the facilitator should field questions and hear from session participants about ideas, areas for further consideration, and any concerns. In preparation for this discussion, the facilitator will lead the group in the co-creation of guiding principles that will make them feel safe, heard, not judged, etc.

Note: *For a more in-depth overview that includes reflective and interactive practices, a certified CBCT teacher is required to facilitate. See "Introductory Offerings" description on page 31 for more information.*

Form the CBCT Committee

Once CBCT for Educators is introduced to members of the community through the orientation session, some may become interested in engaging in the implementation work. This is a great opportunity to invite community members to be a part of the CBCT committee.

Role of the CBCT Committee

The role of the committee will vary depending on the context of the organization and participants. Roles might include:

➡ Exploring and developing expertise in the CBCT concepts and practices

➡ Supporting the implementation process

➡ Reviewing, evaluating, and improving upon the implementation process

➡ Establishing and executing a consistent communication plan to engage community members

Developing and maintaining a CBCT committee helps the implementation process to be inclusive and creates opportunities for members of the education community to be involved and to have a sense of ownership over the work.

Recruit CBCT Committee Members

The makeup of a CBCT committee will vary based on the education system's values, capacity, and community interest levels. Factors that determine the team's composition depend on the size, purpose, and function of the organization. When recruiting CBCT committee members, consider the following steps:

Develop an Inclusive Application Process

▸ Provide an organization-wide application process in which all members of the education community feel invited and included to be involved in the process of CBCT for Educators' planning, piloting, and implementation.

▸ Send out a survey/application to find out who is interested in serving on the committee.

Consider Stakeholders to Invite to Apply

▸ It is beneficial to have someone with decision-making power (such as the school principal, a dean, a district administrator, a department chair, a program coordinator, a provost, etc.) as an active part of the team.

▸ It is recommended that you form a collaborative team that has representation from each stakeholder group or as many of them as possible.

Spread the Word

▸ Use multiple mediums of communication: hallway conversations, staff meetings, emails, etc. If enough interest is developed, consider holding another orientation session to walk through the CBCT for Educators program and implementation process details. See page 20 for orientation session details.

Note: *Use the Organizing and Forming a CBCT Committee Template in Appendix A to identify and organize the CBCT committee. Examples are provided.*

23

CBCT Implementation across Multiple Sites

The approach that successfully implements CBCT for Educators in one school may not work for another school, even within the same region. The process may change from school to school.

If you are scaling CBCT across multiple sites, the recommendation is to work through the process at each site, specifically. Determining readiness factors is a good place to start when developing the process and approach to CBCT implementation. Determining existing assets will support schools in utilizing their current systems, structures, and personnel most effectively.

School Site 1   **School Site 2**

Cental Team

School Site 3   **School Site 4**

This image illustrates a central teaming model. Its make-up includes representation from each school building based CBCT committee.

When implementing CBCT for Educators across multiple sites, we advise forming a central CBCT committee with representation from each school. This team can have similar goals to the individual school-based teams and check in with each other, share ideas, and support each other. The team can also align methods (such as data measurement tools, measuring outcomes, communication and messaging plans, community events, etc.) to support consistency.

Conduct a Stakeholder Audit

In Component 1: Set the Foundation, the needs and readiness of the education system was considered (see page 17). The CBCT committee can now revisit this with a broader network of school or organizational stakeholders. Doing so is beneficial, as it allows schools to gain a better understanding of perspectives and voices among those that are part of the system, supporting the successful implementation of CBCT for Educators.

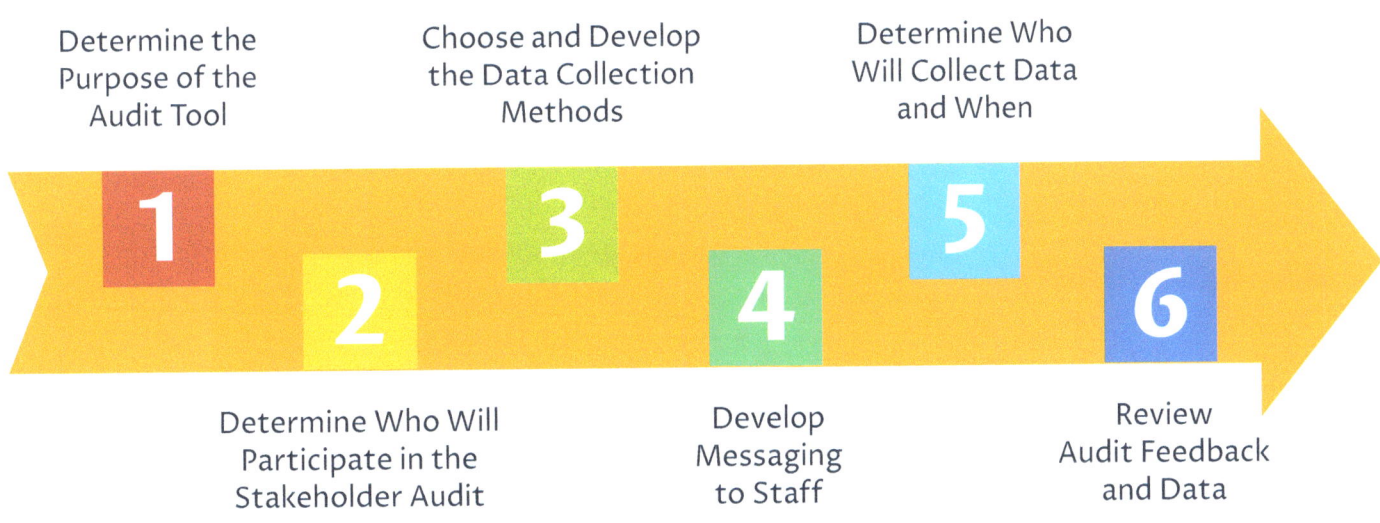

Determine the Purpose of the Audit Tool

Choose and Develop the Data Collection Methods

Determine Who Will Collect Data and When

Determine Who Will Participate in the Stakeholder Audit

Develop Messaging to Staff

Review Audit Feedback and Data

1 Determine the Purpose of the Audit Tool and How the Data Will Be Used

Some of the goals in performing the audit include:

- To assess and understand readiness levels in relation to the integration of CBCT for Educators

- To measure and understand both the assets and needs of the education system

- To identify the school's existing conditions, resources, and factors that can support the success of CBCT for Educators

- To identify possible barriers and challenges to the work and then align CBCT for Educators with areas in need of support

- To gather baseline data to inform the work

- To measure a school community's current levels of buy-in, interest in, and understanding of the program

- To provide stakeholders with an opportunity to voice needs, values, conditions, and support in relation to the CBCT for Educators implementation approach

2 **Determine Who Will Participate in the Stakeholder Audit**

Consider the various stakeholder groups that CBCT for Educators can influence. Feedback from a wide audience of stakeholders, if not all, is recommended. Asking various stakeholders for input establishes the purpose, need, and value for implementing CBCT for Educators. An inclusive process supports engagement, buy-in, and accountability.

3 **Choose and Develop the Data Collection Methods**

- **Survey:** A written or digital survey can be anonymous and helps measure the community's current levels of buy-in, interest in, and understanding of the program. It provides stakeholders with an opportunity to offer feedback regarding implementation needs, values, conditions, and supports. An online survey can be set up with a combination of quantitative and qualitative questions. The quantitative data can be summarized if tools like Google Forms are used, and this does not require a large time commitment or additional resources.

- **Small Group Conversations and Focus Groups:** A voluntary process that includes open-ended questions, which provide more detail and discussion around current readiness levels.

- **Other:** The CBCT committee may choose a different method that better fits their school's needs and context.

Note: *See the Audit Sample Survey in Appendix B to find examples of survey questions.*

4 **Develop Messaging to Staff**

Develop a personal message to staff regarding the purpose and process of the readiness audit.

Example: "As part of our planning and implementation process, we would like to gain feedback from all of you through a readiness audit. This readiness audit will serve as a reflection tool by which the pace and process of CBCT for Educators implementation will be determined. This tool will be used to gain a better understanding of perspectives and voices among those who are part of the system. The purpose of this audit is to ensure an inclusive process, supporting engagement and communication among stakeholders, and to understand the current conditions in the community in relation to integrating CBCT for Educators.

5 Determine Who Will Collect Data and When

If you plan to collect observable and anecdotal data, it is beneficial to have at least two members of the CBCT committee conduct the audit. This mitigates bias and helps conduct a more comprehensive review of the school's conditions for readiness.

Possible times to collect data:

- During a full staff meeting where the program is introduced and time is provided to fill out an anonymous survey.

- Through small group discussions (if you plan to gain anecdotal feedback). Each CBCT committee member can hold data collection meetings or informal conversations with their stakeholder group to gain feedback and understanding and bring it back to the full CBCT committee.

6 Review Audit Feedback and Data

At a CBCT committee meeting, review the full staff and stakeholder data collected from the readiness audit. Through guided discussion, review the data, then identify trends, patterns, needs, and assets. With this information, make recommendations and propose next steps, including how to communicate results to staff and how to align and utilize CBCT for Educators to improve areas in need of attention.

27

Develop and Execute an Outreach and Communication Plan

Note: *Use the Outreach and Communication Plan template in Appendix C to support the development of your outreach and communication plan. An example is provided.*

Once a CBCT committee is established, they will work to develop an outreach and communication plan to inform and engage the community throughout the implementation process. Communication and outreach can take on many forms: email, hallway conversations, staff and faculty meetings, department meetings, etc.

Communication Plan Goals

- Gaining the support of the education system and community

- Sparking interest in CBCT among different stakeholder groups

- Sharing information about different CBCT offerings and practices

- Fostering engagement and interest in CBCT practices and training experiences

Component 3
Offer the Training

Offer the Training

Offer the Training Compassion for Educators course.

Review the Offerings

Make a Plan

Review the Offerings

Training Compassion for Educators is the full CBCT for Educators course. This course involves moving through a sequence of eight modules that each strengthen a particular skill or insight and build on each other to foster greater resilience and compassion.

In some cases, members of the education community may benefit from an introductory experience to give them a sense of the content and practices of CBCT before they begin the full course. All offerings are detailed in this section.

Training Compassion for Educators

Training Compassion for Educators (full course)
(16–24 hours)

Brief Description: A deep dive into the eight CBCT modules, tailored for those who work in education systems. Each module introduces new content, reflective exercises, and practices that are designed to strengthen inner skills and views and to support their application into everyday life.

The Training Compassion for Educators course is offered through Compassion U, a user-friendly app that delivers CBCT course content and provides access to instructional videos, activities, practices, and a compassion community, among other resources.

Courses include live sessions with other participants, facilitated by certified CBCT teachers. These live sessions are typically one hour and occur weekly over the course of nine weeks. Prior to each live session, participants engage in the self-guided content, activities, and practices on Compassion U.

This course can also serve as a prerequisite for those who are interested in applying for the CBCT Teacher Certification program.

Format:

▶ Self-guided on digital learning platform, Compassion U (8–16 hours, typically 1.5 hours per week)

▶ Live sessions in person or via videoconference, facilitated by a certified CBCT teacher (9 hours of live sessions, typically 1 hour per week)

Introductory Offerings

Overview of Training Compassion for Educators
(30 minutes–1.5 hours)

Brief Description: The Overview offered in the Training Compassion for Educators course on Compassion U orients participants to the content and practices of the course. This self-guided experience introduces compassion and compassion training, and includes reflective exercises and practices that set a foundation for the course and give a glimpse into the types of experiences that participants will engage in throughout the rest of the course. The Overview is free and available to anyone through Compassion U.

Format: Fully self-guided on digital learning platform, Compassion U

Introduction to CBCT – Seminar
(45 minutes–3 hours)

Brief Description: An introduction to CBCT, including a sample practice or two. This training provides an overview of CBCT, including an exploration of the framework and history, its benefits for educators, its approach to cultivating resilience and wellbeing, and the science that supports it.

Format: Live session in person or via videoconference, facilitated by a certified CBCT teacher

A Taste of CBCT – Workshop
(4–8 hours)

Brief Description: This workshop exposes participants to the key themes, skills, and insights of the CBCT course, and introduces some of the reflective exercises and informal and formal practices. This workshop provides a taste of the CBCT experience, allowing individuals to begin exploring and strengthening the capacities related to resilience and compassion before diving into the training. This could be done in one long session or broken up into several shorter sessions over multiple days.

Format: Live session(s) in person or via videoconference, facilitated by a certified CBCT teacher

Make a Plan

Want to Bring CBCT to Your School or Organization?

Visit *compassionu. app/ for-organizations*

The path for CBCT for Educators training will change depending on who in the community you are offering it to. For example, a group already on board may dive straight into the full course, meeting weekly over the course of nine weeks. If there is a group that has less time and/or buy in, they may begin with an introductory offering. When making a plan to offer CBCT for Educators, consider the following steps:

"My main takeaway is that this training allows you to work on yourself, and in working on yourself you can then become a greater asset to the people around you (narrow and wide). Building compassion for myself and slowing down to process allows me to be at peace with who I am and my decisions, which translates into being a more compassionate human being."

— EDUCATOR AND CBCT PARTICIPANT

Note: *See Appendix D for a Training Scope template and example.*

1 Determine which group(s) you are bringing CBCT for Educators to.

2 For each group, determine which offering makes most sense to start with (the full course or one of the introductory offerings).

3 Choose an Emory-certified CBCT teacher to facilitate the experience.

4 Determine the format of the training (meeting frequency, length of sessions, online or in person, etc.).

5 Identify date(s) and time(s) the training will take place.

Component 4
Engage in Ongoing Integration

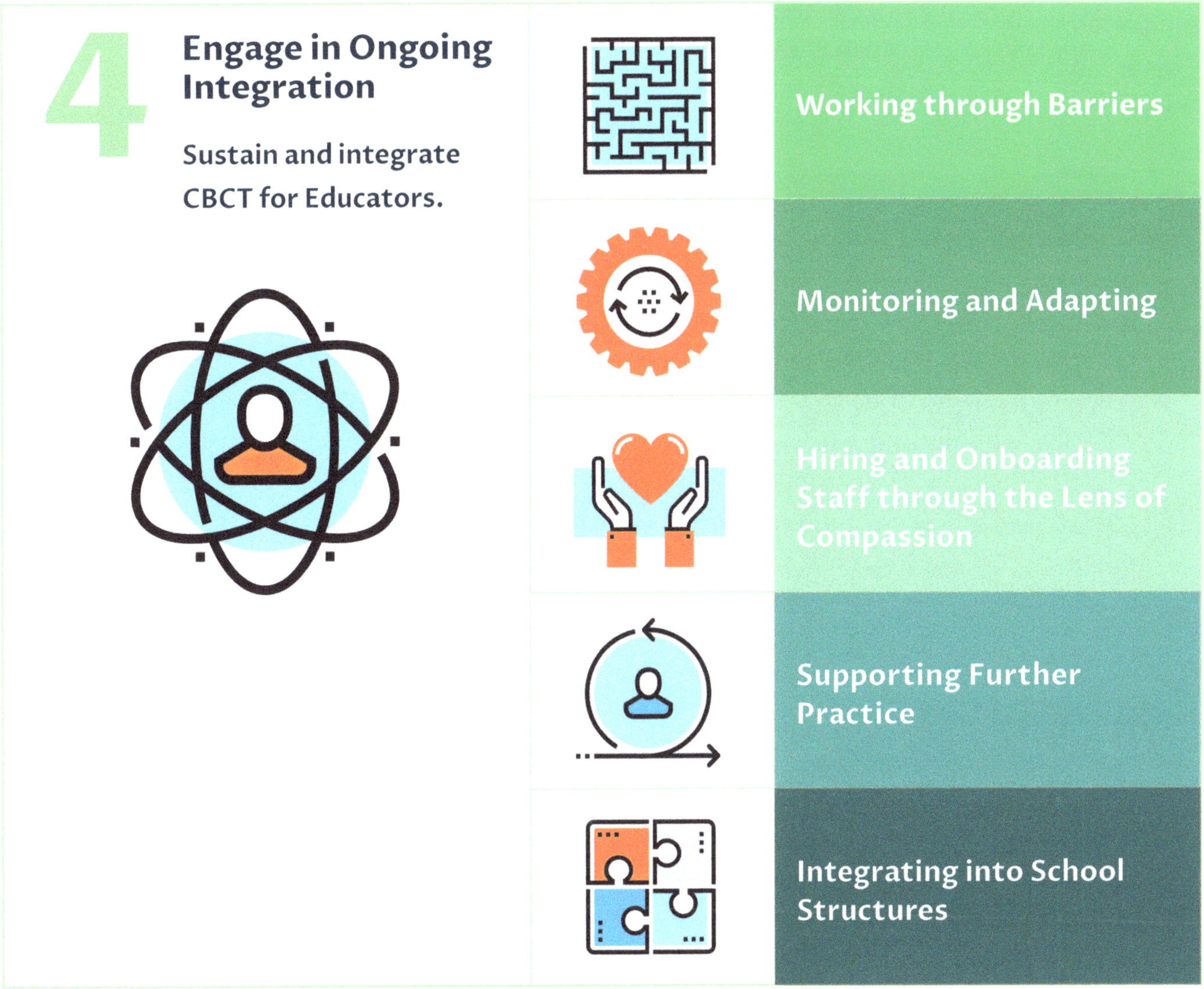

4 Engage in Ongoing Integration

Sustain and integrate CBCT for Educators.

	Working through Barriers
	Monitoring and Adapting
	Hiring and Onboarding Staff through the Lens of Compassion
	Supporting Further Practice
	Integrating into School Structures

 ## Working through Barriers

As anyone who has had the opportunity to lead the implementation of new programs in an education system knows, encountering barriers and challenges is inevitable. Identifying and addressing potential barriers and challenges is key to sustaining meaningful work over time.

Time

- ▶ There is limited time in any education system. Barriers in terms of allocated professional development time are persistent across systems. Prioritization, visible senior support, and long-term planning are key to finding the time for CBCT training.

- ▶ Another successful way to address the issue of time is to deliver the training in bite-sized periods of time; facilitating a 10-minute presentation can lead to interest in a 1-hour session, which may then lead to a half day workshop.

Money

- ▶ Providing compensation for trainings should be considered to support engagement and buy-in. This may be required in certain contexts, depending on the education system, contracts, unions, etc.

- ▶ It is important to prioritize finding the resources and funds to provide introductory offerings to the community, offer the full course to interested members, and support those who would like to engage in the CBCT Teacher Certification program.

- ▶ Identifying sources of funding from grants, the general budget, the professional development budget, or other sources is essential to the planning process.

Buy-in

- ▶ Begin by offering the Training Compassion for Educators course to those who already have buy-in, even if it is a very small group. Have that group report on and share the benefits they experienced with others in the community. Reflecting back the experience and feedback from participants of CBCT from within the system will go a long way in building credibility, fostering authentic engagement, and promoting overall buy-in.

- ▶ Buy-in is also directly related to an effective communication and outreach plan. Helping the education system community to understand the benefits and value-add proposition for them personally and professionally is critical. This can also be done by offering one of the introductory CBCT experiences.

Communication

▶ Education systems often fail to provide consistent and ongoing communication about a prioritized initiative. Through multiple forms and iterations of communication, leaders must voice and message the impact, benefits, and progression of CBCT integration and training throughout the community.

Competing needs

▶ Many initiatives exist within every education system. This is because education systems are required to meet the needs of a wide array of internal and external stakeholders. The ability for CBCT for Educators to be linked and aligned with different initiatives is critical for the success of the overall implementation. Examples of alignment include academic programming/executive functioning, restorative practices, mental health support, and SEL. Regardless of the priority within the education system, it is critical to help faculty and staff see CBCT for Educators as a supportive and aligned effort as opposed to one more thing to add to an already overwhelmed system.

Note: *See the CBCT for Educators Alignment with Education System Initiatives in Appendix E.*

Leadership and staff transition

▶ Leadership and staff transition are inevitable. Establishing a strong culture and climate that is characterized by resilience, awareness, and compassion will ensure that the transition of key staff does not undermine efforts to further CBCT for Educators programming, training, and integration.

Monitoring and Adapting

Feedback on how the program is being received is essential for the program's success and for maintaining the sustained buy-in of faculty and staff. Maintaining a sense of how the program is being received relies on ongoing monitoring. Feedback can come in the form of written feedback, formal and informal conversations, and classroom-based observations with students. Each of these forms of feedback provides the education system's leadership with insights into the impacts that CBCT for Educators programming has on the faculty and staff. One important pathway for feedback can (and should) occur through the CBCT committee. As a representative committee, this group can engage faculty and staff stakeholders to gain meaningful insights about the experience of CBCT for Educators within the education system.

After reviewing this feedback, the CBCT committee can develop recommendations to adapt and improve the program's implementation. This may mean providing additional training, enhancing external communication, creating a committee that is representative of all stakeholders within the educational system, or developing new integration strategies for CBCT practices and related activities.

 ## Hiring and Onboarding Staff through the Lens of Compassion

Integrating CBCT for Educators into a school's culture depends on the members of that school's community. The hiring and onboarding of new staff provides a key pathway for CBCT for Educators integration.

When hiring new staff at the school, consider seeking out candidates who have knowledge and/or experience that correlates with a CBCT approach, including trauma-informed teaching; restorative practices and pedagogy; diversity, equity, and inclusion framework; and SEL. The applicant's letter of interest, resume, and interview should offer evidence of their interests, experience, and accomplishments in these areas. The selection of applicants who practice resilience and compassion goes a long way in sustaining a resilient and compassionate school culture.

When onboarding new staff, introduce CBCT for Educators in the new-staff orientation and through mentorship.

- **Orientation:** The orientation is a great opportunity to introduce the program and begin to engage in its practices. This is an opportunity for the school's leadership to prioritize and highlight the culture of compassion they are working to embed.

- **Mentorship:** Under the guidance of skilled mentors with a high level of CBCT knowledge, new staff can better understand and benefit from the culture of compassion and feel motivated to engage in the initiative or learn more about it.

 ## Supporting Further Practice

Certifying Community Members in CBCT

One of the best and most sustainable ways to ensure supported and ongoing implementation of CBCT for Educators is to provide pathways for interested staff and faculty to become certified CBCT teachers.

Each year, Emory's Compassion Center accepts a new cohort of experienced practitioners to enroll in the six-month CBCT Teacher Certification program, which is designed to provide high-quality instruction of CBCT for research purposes, as well as the general sharing of the CBCT skills and content with a wider audience.

Emory's Compassion Center is committed to fostering compassion and ethics in education. Different scholarship opportunities exist within the Center and beyond to offset the costs of CBCT Teacher Certification.

Encouraging Continued Practice

Once groups in the community complete the Training Compassion for Educators course, it is important to have structures in place for them to continue engaging in and deepening their practice, individually and in the community. Interested faculty and staff can join existing communities of CBCT practice so that they feel supported and receive access to guided CBCT practices. As the education system gains capacity through training its staff and faculty as certified CBCT teachers, it can also establish a regular community of practice to support the deepening and continuity of CBCT practices within the school community.

Encouraging Staff/Faculty to Become Certified CBCT Teachers

▶ Offer regular Training Compassion for Educators courses. This is a prerequisite for the CBCT Teacher Certification program.

▶ Share the following information about the CBCT Teacher Certification program with members interested in the implementation of CBCT in their school(s).

■ Opportunities / benefits of certification

- Ability to teach CBCT to educators and administrators (in their community and beyond), and to members of the general public

- Access to a global compassion community of other certified CBCT instructors (educators and individuals in other sectors)

- Deepened familiarity with the content and practices of CBCT and enhanced personal wellbeing

■ Funding / Scholarship opportunities available to them (if applicable)

■ Certification process details (visit *compassionu.app/teacher-certification* for this information)

"Becoming a CBCT instructor has impacted me personally, socially, and professionally. The time I spent reflecting on the CBCT practices added solace to my day, insights into problem solving with compassion, and most importantly self-care."

— EDUCATOR AND CERTIFIED CBCT INSTRUCTOR

Encouraging Individual Practice

The CBCT for Educators practices, while often done in community, are personal practices aimed at strengthening a participant's inner skills and capacities. This inner work is not complete in one, five, or even one hundred courses, but rather is understood as a lifelong practice—something we all continue to engage in, train, and apply throughout our lives. Finding the time and space to engage in the practices and incorporate them into our busy schedules and existing routines is a challenge.

Encouraging and enabling these practices in the educator community can make participants more likely to engage and can make them feel supported, nourished, and motivated. Consider the following ways to encourage individual practice:

✓ Provide subscriptions to Compassion U for interested faculty and staff

✓ Create a physical space on campus for relaxation and contemplative practice

✓ Integrate CBCT practice within the existing wellness and health programming offered

✓ Establish a community of practice for interested members of the education community

✓ Embed services provided by Compassion U into an existing or emerging staff and faculty mentoring program

Encouraging Group Practice

Communities of practice

The CBCT committee can provide options for people to participate in a community of practice once they have completed the Training Compassion for Educators course. Individual groups may also choose to form their own communities of practice. Each community of practice may choose to focus on different elements of the practice. They may meet regularly to:

- ▶ **Debrief the modules in sequence:** Going through the modules together, taking time on their own to engage in the formal and informal practices, and then debriefing together in the group.
- ▶ **Engage in insight activities:** Revisiting the insight activities from the course, engaging in them as a group, and then debriefing.
- ▶ **Engage in formal practices:** Engaging in the formal practices as a group.
- ▶ **Share and apply:** Engaging in informal sharing about which CBCT for Educators skills and insights have been most meaningful or most challenging for them in their work recently.

Mentoring and accountability groups

Mentoring and accountability groups can support continued practice and build connections within the community. These groups (or pairs) can come together to support, encourage, and motivate each other to commit to ongoing practice and application of the CBCT for Educators skills into their daily lives. For example, at the start of each month, participants in these small groups might review the informal practice section of a chosen module and select one or more they plan to bring into their lives that month. They can share what they have chosen to work on with their accountability partner(s) and check in periodically throughout the month on their progress, insights, and challenges.

Integrating into Education System Structures

Implementing CBCT for Educators into the school's culture goes beyond personal and group practice. It also involves integration of the practices and principles of CBCT into the systems, routines, and structures of the community.

Identify optimal times to integrate key practices and principles of CBCT for Educators into routines and structures.

"I wish more schools were willing to make this a part of orientation or a teacher work day."

— EDUCATOR

Incorporate CBCT for Educators into an orientation.

Incorporate CBCT settling practices into meetings.

Share updates on implementation work in staff/faculty meetings.

Work CBCT into the annual evaluation process (especially the focus on self-compassion).

Offer CBCT courses to other constituencies (parents, partner schools or organizations, the school board, or system administrators).

Apply compassion-based ethics to the institution's disciplinary policies and/or to classroom management or behavior management strategies.

Bring the compassion-based sister program, SEE Learning, to the school as an SEL program (refer to page 8 for more information).

Note: *When CBCT practices and activities are applied in a group setting, individuals should be given a choice and options regarding if and how they participate.*

40

Conclusion

Educating students at any level, from preschool to university, represents a challenging task. Reconciling the seemingly infinite range of student needs with limited resources is difficult at best. Coupling this reality with more extreme mental health and behavioral issues manifesting in students has led to a troubling situation for educators.

Although educators may not always be able to change these external circumstances in the short term, they can engage in practices that foster a greater degree of wellbeing, compassion, and resilience among those in their education system.

In this guide, we walked through a step-by-step process for implementing CBCT for Educators into an education system. The process outlined here represents a realistic approach, based on others' experiences and best practices within education, and allows for variation and adaptation. No two education systems are the same, and how CBCT for Educators is implemented will need to be continuously and creatively reconsidered to encourage each community's buy-in, commitment, and sustained engagement.

For those who embark on this meaningful journey, know that the Emory Compassion Center will be there to support you as much as possible, and that there is a growing network of others across the world—schools and school systems, administrators, teachers, parents, researchers, and others—who are pioneers in the field of compassion and education. As the network grows, the potential of each individual organization to make a difference will also grow. With sustained effort and mutual support, this work can contribute to a more compassionate and ethical world for all.

Keep In Touch

Visit:
compassionu. app/ for-organizations

Email:
partnerships. cbct@emory.edu

Appendix A

Organizing and Forming a CBCT Committee (Template)

CBCT Committee

Meeting Dates and Time:

CBCT Committee Member	Stakeholder Group	Communication Method
Who will serve on the CBCT committee?	Which stakeholder group will they represent?	When will they give information to their stakeholder group? *Suggested: monthly one-hour meeting*

Determine the purpose and goals of the team:

Organizing and Forming a CBCT Committee: Elementary School Example

CBCT Committee
Meeting Dates and Time: Every third Thursday of the month from 3–4 P.M.

CBCT Committee Member Who will serve on the CBCT committee?	Stakeholder Group Which stakeholder group will they represent?	Communication Method When will they give information to their stakeholder group?
Certified CBCT teacher	CBCT Core Committee	Monthly CBCT committee meeting
Mr. Brown (K teacher)	Teachers PK–K	Monthly planning meeting
Ms. June (Grade 1 teacher)	Teachers Grades 1–2	Monthly planning meeting
Ms. Jones (Grade 4 teacher)	Teachers Grades 3–4	Monthly lunch-and-learn session
Dr. Anderson (School Counselor)	Counselors and school psychologists	Monthly student intervention meeting
Mr. Tenzin (Specialty Teacher)	Specialty area teachers (art, world languages, etc.)	Monthly lunch-and-learn with specialty area teachers
Hally Berry	Parent who serves on the parent–teacher organization	Monthly parent–teacher meeting
Georgio T.	Student who serves on the youth voice team or student council	Monthly youth voice team/ student council meeting

Determine the purpose and goals of the team:

1. Explore and develop expertise in CBCT for Educators concepts and practices.

   ▪ As a team, engage in and reflect on CBCT for Educators practices.

- Reflect on personal and professional growth and share findings with the larger school community.

- Provide support and/or coordinate professional learning and opportunities for faculty and staff.

2. Support identified trainings and implementation processes. Examples can include piloting a small group of teachers, establishing a grade-level community of practice, developing a mentoring program, etc.

   - Build upon strengths and develop creative ideas to support progress and address any barriers and challenges.

   - Share implementation's successes and challenges.

   - Provide guidance on topics and activities.

3. Collect, review, and utilize feedback data to understand implementation's progress.

4. Establish a consistent communication plan.

Organizing and Forming a CBCT Committee: Secondary School Example

CBCT Committee

Meeting Dates and Time: Every third Thursday of the month from 3–4 P.M.

CBCT Committee Member Who will serve on the CBCT committee?	Stakeholder Group Which stakeholder group will they represent?	Communication Method When will they give information to their stakeholder group?
Certified CBCT teacher	CBCT Core Committee	Monthly CBCT committee meeting
Mr. Brown (counselor)	Counselors and school psychologists	Monthly student intervention meeting
Ms. June (language arts and literature)	Teachers of language arts and literature	Monthly planning meeting
Ms. Jones (math)	Teachers of math	Monthly lunch-and-learn session
Mr. Tenzin (SLP)	Specialty area teachers (art, industrial arts, world language, etc.)	Monthly lunch and planning session with specialty area teachers
Hally Berry	Parent who serves on the parent–teacher organization	Monthly parent–teacher meeting
Georgio T.	Student who serves on the youth voice team or student council	Monthly youth voice team/ student council meeting

Determine the purpose and goals of the team:

1. Explore and develop expertise in CBCT for Educators concepts and practices.

   ▪ As a team, engage in and reflect on CBCT for Educators practices.

- Reflect on personal and professional growth and share findings with the larger school community.

- Provide support and/or coordinate professional learning and opportunities for faculty and staff.

2. Support identified trainings and implementation processes. Examples can include piloting a small group of teachers, establishing a grade-level community of practice, developing or using an existing mentoring program structure, etc.

   - Build upon strengths and develop creative ideas to support progress and address any barriers and challenges.

   - Share implementation's successes and challenges.

   - Provide guidance on topics and activities.

3. Collect, review, and utilize feedback data to understand implementation's progress.

4. Establish a consistent communication plan.

Organizing and Forming a CBCT Committee: Higher Education Example

CBCT Committee

Meeting Dates and Time: Every third Thursday of the month from 3–4 P.M.

CBCT committee Member Who will serve on the CBCT committee?	Stakeholder Group Which stakeholder group will they represent?	Communication Method When will they give information to their stakeholder group?
Certified CBCT teacher	CBCT Core Committee	Monthly CBCT committee meeting
Dr. Brown (Chemistry Department, College of Science, and faculty senate representative)	Faculty and representative from faculty senate	Monthly faculty meeting and faculty senate session
Dr. June (Curriculum Department and College of Education)	Faculty	Monthly department and quarterly college faculty and staff meetings
VP of Human Resources (HR Department)	Leadership	Monthly leadership meeting
Mr. Tenzin (staff development coordinator)	Staff	Monthly planning session with staff development providers
Hally Berry	Community advisory committee member	Monthly committee meeting
Georgio T.	Student senate representative who serves on the youth voice team or student council	Monthly youth voice team/student council meeting

Determine the purpose and goals of the team:

1. Explore and develop expertise in CBCT for Educators concepts and practices.

   - As a team, engage in and reflect on CBCT for Educators practices.

- Reflect on personal and professional growth and share findings with the larger school community.

- Provide support and/or coordinate professional learning and opportunities for faculty and staff.

2. Support identified trainings and implementation processes. Examples can include piloting a small group of teachers, establishing a grade-level community of practice, developing a mentoring program, etc.

   - Build upon strengths and develop creative ideas to support progress and address any barriers and challenges.

   - Share implementation's successes and challenges.

   - Provide guidance on topics and activities.

3. Collect, review, and utilize feedback data to understand implementation's progress.

4. Establish a consistent communication plan.

Appendix B

Audit Sample Survey

Understanding, Interest, and Motivation

1. Please rate how familiar you are with CBCT for Educators.

1	**2**	**3**	**4**	**5**
not at all	*a little*	*somewhat*	*mostly*	*very much*

2. How do you understand compassion and its value both personally and professionally?

3. Please rate how often you apply compassion in your daily life

1	**2**	**3**	**4**	**5**
not at all	*a little*	*somewhat*	*mostly*	*very much*

4. How do you understand self-compassion and its value both personally and professionally?

5. Please rate how often you apply self-compassion in your daily life.

1	**2**	**3**	**4**	**5**
not at all	*a little*	*somewhat*	*mostly*	*very much*

6. How interested are you to learn more about CBCT for Educators?

1	**2**	**3**	**4**	**5**
not at all	*a little*	*somewhat*	*mostly*	*very much*

7. How much, if at all, do you believe incorporating CBCT for Educators into our school will have a positive impact?

1	**2**	**3**	**4**	**5**
not at all	*a little*	*somewhat*	*mostly*	*very much*

Understanding, Interest, and Motivation   *(continued)*

8. How motivated are you to support the implementation of CBCT for Educators into our school?

1	**2**	**3**	**4**	**5**
not at all	*a little*	*somewhat*	*mostly*	*very much*

9. What would you hope to get out of this program (professionally/personally, short-term/long-term, etc.)?

Culture and Current Conditions

10. We are providing a safe, healthy, and effective learning environment for our students.

1	**2**	**3**	**4**	**5**
not at all	*a little*	*somewhat*	*mostly*	*very much*

11. The administration provides a safe, healthy, and effective environment for professional success.

1	**2**	**3**	**4**	**5**
not at all	*a little*	*somewhat*	*mostly*	*very much*

12. The administration supports a strong compassionate culture at our school.

1	**2**	**3**	**4**	**5**
not at all	*a little*	*somewhat*	*mostly*	*very much*

13. I see a need for a stronger culture of compassion at our school.

1	**2**	**3**	**4**	**5**
not at all	*a little*	*somewhat*	*mostly*	*very much*

14. What preexisting programs or structures, if any, can be built upon to support the implementation of CBCT for Educators in our school?

1	**2**	**3**	**4**	**5**
not at all	*a little*	*somewhat*	*mostly*	*very much*

15. What barriers, if any, may hinder the integration of CBCT for Educators in our school?

Appendix C

Outreach and Communication Plan (Template)

Topic	Method of Communication and Frequency	By Whom

Outreach and Communication Plan Example

Topic	Method of Communication and Frequency	By Whom
About the initiative	Monthly newsletter—a short write up and/or photograph highlighting the work	CBCT committee member
Invitation to participate (multiple times and in multiple ways)	Monthly—at the start or end of a staff meeting, hallway conversations, and check-ins	CBCT committee members
Updates on the training and piloting	Monthly—communicating to the staff at a monthly meeting and in a newsletter	CBCT committee members
Audit purpose and process, including sharing results	Purpose and process—the start of a full staff meeting in November Share results—one full staff meeting in January	CBCT committee members
Outcomes of the training experience and piloting	Monthly—communicating to the staff at a monthly meeting and in a newsletter	CBCT committee members
Celebrations	Shout-outs during full staff meetings, individualized emails, check-ins, and informal ongoing conversations	CBCT committee members

Appendix D

Training Scope (Template)

	Year 1	Year 2	Year 3
Introduction to CBCT – Seminar			
A Taste of CBCT – Workshop			
Training Compassion for Educators course			
CBCT Teacher Certification program			

Training Scope Example

	Year 1	Year 2	Year 3
Introduction to CBCT – Seminar	All staff during an inservice day	Community members and families during a family information night or parent–teacher meeting	New staff and community member refresher
A Taste of CBCT – Workshop	Group in the school community that expresses interest but is not ready to dive into the full training yet	New staff during new staff orientation	All staff during inservice days or at a monthly faculty meeting
Training Compassion for Educators course	CBCT committee, and early adopter group in the school that already has buy-in	Group that participated in the workshop in Year 1 now ready to take the full course and other interested groups ready to dive right into the training	New staff from Year 2, now ready to take the full course
CBCT Teacher Certification program	Lead coordinator/ teacher	School counselor	Lead coordinator/ teacher

Appendix E

CBCT for Educators Alignment with Education System Initiatives

Academic Programming/Executive Functioning

- The goal of most education systems is the achievement of academic excellence in each student. Supporting academic success often relies on the development of skills and competencies that go beyond cognitive aptitude. Other factors that influence academic achievement are students' abilities to navigate adversity with resilience, foster impulse control, regulate their nervous system during times of stress and adversity, and recognize the perspectives of others. As an academic intervention, students' abilities to form secure and trusting relationships with their educators consistently ranks as having one of the strongest effects corresponding to academic outcomes. CBCT for Educators fosters competencies in participants that help them to foster and strengthen relationships that are imbued with tenderness, care, and compassion.

SEL Implementation

- CASEL plays a pivotal role in advancing the SEL field by identifying high-quality SEL programs and creating a designation for research-based programs with real impact. Over 25 years, CASEL has advocated strongly for adult SEL in order to effectively implement SEL programs and overcome the factors contributing to and the symptoms of educator burnout. CBCT stands out as the most research-backed compassion training available. CBCT for Educators provides SEL for adults, enhancing teacher wellness and effectiveness in implementing SEE Learning.

Restorative Practices

- Restorative practice is a research-based approach that serves to address behavioral issues and conflicts. Through a simple and easy-to-use protocol, individuals or groups of people who experience conflict can establish a procedure for communication and restoration. Restorative practice is grounded in four key principles: Relationships, Responsibility, Reparation, and Resilience. The Enduring Capabilities and practice developed through the Training Compassion for Educators course enhance and support each of these key areas by building applied and ready-to-use skills such as perspective taking, sustained attention, awareness of thoughts and feelings, nervous system regulation, a sense of shared common humanity, and compassion. CBCT for Educators builds and reinforces many of the interpersonal and compassion-based skills needed to be an effective practitioner and facilitator of restorative practices.

Wellness Programming and Mental Health Supports

- Education systems are struggling with unprecedented mental health issues amongst faculty, staff, and students. The mental health crisis is a global issue and has grown in scope and intensity in recent years. As a research-based program, CBCT has demonstrated impact and benefit in addressing mental health issues and burnout-related symptoms. CBCT provides applied tools and practices that foster a sense of purpose, attentional stability and self-awareness, and compassion for the self and others. The alignment of CBCT practices with current mental health support and wellness programming provides an evidence base for the efforts being developed and implemented to foster a more caring and compassionate culture and climate.

Appendix F

Sample Five Year Path: Implementing CBCT for Educators in Your School

Year 1	Exploration of CBCT for Educators
Month	**Sample Path**
July	Educator Sandy hears about CBCT for Educators, perhaps through awareness of the SEE Learning curriculum or other initiatives occurring at the Center for Contemplative Science and Compassion-Based Ethics at Emory University.
September	Sandy signs up at Compassion U and tries the free Overview module.
October	Sandy is inspired to enroll in CBCT for the general public via the app. After a few weeks, she notices that she is better managing her emotional life and thus her classroom as well. She has an "aha" moment: SEL is not just for students!
December	Sandy begins to tell her colleagues about the course, and she hears that one of the administrators, Alex, is already interested in meditation. She approaches him about CBCT for Educators, and he seems interested and asks what it costs.
January	Sandy and Alex reach out to the Emory Compassion Center to set up a course for their faculty and staff with an experienced, certified CBCT teacher. The administrator identifies resources from professional development funds to cover the training costs, while Sandy prepares a 10-minute presentation for her faculty meeting using template slides provided by the Emory Compassion Center.
February	The first course runs from February to April. Though only six people sign up, the diverse group enjoys it and forms new collegial bonds in the process, across departments.
March	Sandy and a colleague from another department, Zoe, decide they want to be certified CBCT teachers. They apply for the program and for scholarships to cover what they cannot afford or has not been provided by the education system.
April	The post-course evaluations are promising. The word spreads that the course is helpful. Messages are sent through email and other media to share updates about the benefits and impacts of the CBCT for Educators training program.
May	Sandy and Zoe begin the Teacher Certification program, with intensive study through the summer.

Year 2 — Building Capacity to Deliver CBCT for Educators

Month	Sample Path
July	Sandy and Zoe plan their first course, which will be supervised by Emory University as part of their certification process. They advertise to colleagues and present about CBCT at the start-of-year faculty meeting.
September	Eighteen people sign up to take Sandy and Zoe's course, which is run through the CompassionU app. The administration funds each participant's use of the app from professional development funds, and the teaching portion is free because Sandy and Zoe are donating their time as teachers-in-training.
October	The CBCT committee is established to understand related initiatives and efforts, such as promoting a positive culture and climate, etc.
December	The SEL specialist at the school or the wellness coordinator at the university is enrolled in the CBCT course and becomes interested in the Emory Compassion Center's sister program for students: SEE Learning. This leads to a multi-year relationship with SEE Learning for student-focused programming.
January	Post-course evaluations show promise. Sandy and Zoe create a compassion board in the main hall to showcase and celebrate efforts to foster and promote compassion amongst educators and students. Some classes begin to use CBCT practices and SEE Learning, and terms such as "empathy," "gratitude," and "emotional-" and "systems intelligence" are percolating through the school. Compassion becomes better understood and appreciated by all.
February	Another round of CBCT is advertised for the spring. This time, 40 people sign up for 20 slots, so there is a wait list. Two more educators express interest in doing the teacher certification the following summer.
March	As Year 2 progresses, more senior leaders and community partners – such as parents, neighboring administrators, district-level human resources staff, and psychologists – begin to show an interest in CBCT.
April	Two more educators enroll in the teacher certification with Emory. A small group of educators meet early each morning to practice CBCT together.
May	The CBCT committee presents recommendations for CBCT programming, training, and integration to the school leaders and teachers.

Year 3 — Implementing CBCT across the Education System

Month	Sample Path
July	Faculty orientation includes compassion-related exercises, themes, and meditations.
October	The CBCT committee reviews approved recommendations for programming, training, and integration to develop an action plan for implementation.
November	More courses are taught throughout the year. The CBCT for Educators' recommendations are enacted. The CBCT five-minute settling practice becomes the standard way to start a faculty meeting.

Year 4 — Understanding and Strengthening CBCT for Educators' Implementation

Month	Sample Path
July	Compassion training skills and competencies are brought to bear on education system-wide policies, including disciplinary procedures, student assessment, and employee evaluations. The education system begins to attract educators who appreciate the value of compassion and compassion training.

Year 5 — Embedding CBCT for Educators among All Staff and Faculty

Month	Sample Path
July	CBCT becomes part of onboarding for all new faculty and staff. The long-term impacts of investing in compassion training become apparent in the education system culture. Regular leadership training is provided to support a compassionate culture and climate.

Notes

1   Turner, D. M., Aljure, I., & Canevari, P. (2016, April 1). 7 powerful actions you can take to improve relationships with your students. Brain Based Learning, Brain Based Experts. http://www.brainbasedlearning.net/improve-relationships-with-students/

2. Pace, T. W. W., Negi, L. T., Adame, D. D., Cole, S. P., Sivilli, T. I., Brown, T. D., Issa, M. J., & Raison, C. L. (2009). Effect of compassion meditation on neuroendocrine, innate immune and behavioral responses to psychosocial stress. *Psychoneuroendocrinology,* 34(1), 87–98. https://doi.org/10.1016/j.psyneuen.2008.08.011; Pace, T., Negi, L., Donaldson-Lavelle, B., Ozawa-de Silva, B., Reddy, S., Cole, S., Craighead, L., & Raison, C. (2012). Cognitively-Based Compassion Training reduces peripheral inflammation in adolescents in foster care with high rates of early life adversity. *BMC Complementary and Alternative Medicine*, 12(Suppl 1), 175. https://doi.org/10.1186%2F1472-6882-12-S1-P175; Pace, T. W. W., Negi, L. T., Dodson-Lavelle, B., Ozawa-de Silva, B., Reddy, S. D., Cole, S. P., Danese, A., Craighead, L. W., & Raison, C. L. (2013). Engagement with Cognitively-Based Compassion Training is associated with reduced salivary C-reactive protein from before to after training in foster care program adolescents. *Psychoneuroendocrinology*, 38(2), 294–299. https://doi.org/10.1016/j.psyneuen.2012.05.019; Reddy, S., Negi, L., Dodson-Lavelle, B., Ozawa-de Silva, B., Pace, T., Cole, S., Raison, C., & Craighead, L. (2013). Cognitive-based compassion training: A promising prevention strategy for at-risk adolescents. *Journal of Child and Family Studies*, 22(2), 219–230. http://dx.doi.org/10.1007/s10826-012-9571-7; Titanji, B. K., Tejani, M., Farber, E. W., Mehta, C. C., Pace, T. W., Meagley, K., Gavegnano, C., Harrison, T., Kokubun, C. W., Negi, S. D., Schinazi, R. F., & Marconi, V. C. (2022). Cognitively Based Compassion Training for HIV immune nonresponders—An attention-placebo randomized controlled trial. *Journal of Acquired Immune Deficiency Syndromes*, 89(3), 340–348. https://doi.org/10.1097/QAI.0000000000002874.

3. Lang, A. J., Casmar, P., Hurst, S., Harrison, T., Golshan, S., Good, R., Essex, M., & Negi, L. (2017). Compassion meditation for veterans with posttraumatic stress disorder (PTSD): A nonrandomized study. Mindfulness, 11(1), 63–74. https://doi.org/10.1007/s12671-017-0866-z; Mascaro, J. S., Kelley, S., Darcher, A., Negi, L. T., Worthman, C., Miller, A., & Raison, C. (2016). Meditation buffers medical student compassion from the deleterious effects of depression. *Journal of Positive Psychology,* 13(2), 133–142. https://doi.org/10.1080/17439760.2016.1233348.

4. Mascaro, J. S. et al. (2016).

5. Lang, A. J. et al. (2017).

6. Reddy, S. et al. (2013).

7. Desbordes, G., Negi, L. T., Pace, T. W., Wallace, B. A., Raison, C. L., & Schwartz. E. L. (2012). Effects of mindful-attention and compassion meditation training on amygdala response to emotional stimuli in an ordinary, non-meditative state. *Frontiers in Human Neuroscience*, 6, 292. https://doi.org/10.3389/fnhum.2012.00292; Mascaro, J. S. et al. (2016).

8. Mascaro, J., Rilling, J., Negi, L. T., & Raison, C. (2012). Compassion meditation enhances empathic accuracy and related neural activity. *Social Cognitive and Affective Neuroscience*, 8(1), 48–55. https://doi.org/10.1093/scan/nss095.

9. Gonzalez-Hernandez, E., Romero, R., Campos, D., Burychka, D., Diego-Pedro, R., Baños, R., Negi, L., & Cebolla, A. (2018). Cognitively-Based Compassion Training (CBCT) in breast cancer survivors: A randomized clinical trial study. *Integrative Cancer Therapies*, 17(3), 684–696. https://doi.org/10.1177/1534735418772095; Sun, S., Pickover, A. M., Goldberg, S. B., Bhimji, J., Nguyen, J. K., Evans, A. E., Patterson, B., & Kaslow, N. J. (2019). For whom does Cognitively Based Compassion Training (CBCT) work? An analysis of predictors and moderators among African American suicide attempters. *Mindfulness*, 10(11), 2327–2340. https:// doi.org/10.1007/s12671-019-01207-6; Titanji, B. K. et al., (2022)

10. Gonzalez-Hernandez, E., Romero, R., Campos, D., Burychka, D., Diego-Pedro, R., Baños, R., Negi, L., & Cebolla, A. (2018). Cognitively-Based Compassion Training (CBCT) in breast cancer survivors: A randomized clinical trial study. *Integrative Cancer Therapies*, 17(3), 684–696. https://doi.org/10.1177/1534735418772095; Sun, S., Pickover, A. M., Goldberg, S. B., Bhimji, J., Nguyen, J. K., Evans, A. E., Patterson, B., & Kaslow, N. J. (2019). For whom does Cognitively Based Compassion Training (CBCT) work? An analysis of predictors and moderators among African American suicide attempters. *Mindfulness*, 10(11), 2327–2340. https:// doi.org/10.1007/s12671-019-01207-6; Titanji, B. K. et al., (2022).

11. United Nations (2024). Secretary-General's video message to launch the Report of the High-Level Panel on the Teaching Profession. https://www.un.org/sg/en/content/sg/statement/2024-02-26/secretary-generals-video-message-launch-the-report-of-the-high-level-panel-the-teaching-profession

12. Ingersoll, R. M., & Tran, H. (2023). Teacher shortages and turnover in rural schools in the U.S.: An organizational analysis. *Educational Administration Quarterly*, 59(2), 396–431. https://doi.org/10.1177/0013161X231159922

13. Shuls, J. V., & Flores, J. M. (2020). Improving teacher retention through support and development. *Journal of Educational Leadership and Policy Studies*, 4(1), 1–19.

14. Aucejo, E. M., & Romano, T. F. (2016). Assessing the effect of school days and absences on test score performance. *Economics of Education Review*, 55, 70–87.

15. Liu, J., Lee, M., & Gershenson, S. (2021). The short- and long-run impacts of secondary school absences. *Journal of Public Economics*, 199.

16. Binder, A. J., & Bound, J. (2019). The declining labor market prospects of less-educated men. *Journal of Economic Perspectives*, 33(2), 163–190.

17. Allison, M. A., Attisha, E., & Council on School Health (2019). The link between school attendance and good health. *Pediatrics*, 143(2), e20183648.

18. Lochner, L., & Moretti, E. (2004). The effect of education on crime: Evidence from prison inmates, arrests, and self-reports. *The American Economic Review*, 94(1), 155–189.

19. Gottfried, M., Kim, P., & Fletcher, T. L. (2024). Do teachers perceive absent students differently? AERA Open, 10. https://doi.org/10.1177/23328584241259398

20. Jaciw, A. P., Wingard, A., Zacamy, J., Lin, L., & Lau, S. (2021). *Final Report of the i3 Evaluation o Collaboration and Reflection to Enhance Atlanta Teacher Effectiveness (CREATE) Teacher Residency Program: A Qua ExperimenT, Georgia*. (Empirical Education Rep. No. Empirical_GSU-7031-FR1-2021-0.1). Empirical Education Inc. https://www.empiricaleducation.com/create/